KU-865-518

A WORLD OF FESTIVALS

PASSOVER

David Rose
and
Gill Rose

Evans Brothers Limited

Published by Evans Brothers Limited
2A Portman Mansions
Chiltern Street
London W1U 6NR

VISIT OUR WEBSITE
Evans
www.evansbooks.co.uk

© copyright Evans Brothers Limited 1997
First published 1997
Reprinted 1998
First published in paperback 2000. Reprinted 2003, 2004, 2005

All Rights Reserved. No part of this publication may
be reproduced, stored in a retrieval system or
transmitted in any form, or by any means, electronic,
mechanical, photocopying, recording or otherwise,
without prior permission of Evans Brothers Limited.

British Library Cataloguing in Publication data.
A catalogue record for this book is available from the
British Library.

Printed in Spain by G.Z. Printek

ISBN 0 237 52861 4

ACKNOWLEDGEMENTS

Editor: Su Swallow
Design: Neil Sayer
Production: Jenny Mulvanny

The authors and publishers would like to thank Anne
Clark for her help and support in the preparation of
this text, and the staff and children of the
Independent Jewish Day School, London, for their
help and cooperation in the making of some of the
images in this book.

For permission to reproduce copyright material, the
authors and publishers gratefully acknowledge the
following;

Cover: Circa Photo Library/Barrie Searle
Title page: Trip/H Rogers
Contents page: Trip/H Rogers
page 6 David Rose **page 7** (top) David Rose,
(bottom) Zefa **page 8** Trip/H Rogers **page 9** David
Rose **page 10** (top) Nancy Durrell McKenna/Panos
Pictures, (bottom) Robert Harding Picture Library
page 11 (top) Liba Taylor/Hutchison Library,
(bottom) David Rose **page 12** Ancient Art and
Architecture Collection, (bottom) Trip/H Rogers
page 13 David Rose **page 14** (top) Trip/Muzlish,
(bottom) David Rose **page 15** Ancient Art and
Architecture **page 16** (top) Trip/P Mitchell, (bottom)
Trip/H Rogers **page 17** Ancient Art and Architecture
page 18 Zefa **page 19** (top) David Rose, (bottom)
Circa Photo Library/Barrie Searle **page 20/21** David
Rose **page 22** Trip/M Jenkin **page 23** (top) Liba
Taylor/Hutchison Library, (bottom) David Rose **page
24** Micheal J O'Brien/Panos Pictures **page 25** (left)
Ancient Art and Architecture, (right) David Rose
page 26 (left) Angela Silvertop/Hutchison Library,
(right) Nancy Durrell McKenna/Hutchison Library
page 27 David Rose **28/29** Alan Towse Photography

83746

SOUTH DEVON COLLEGE LIBRARY

PASSOVER

JON COLLEGE LI

WITHDRAWN

SOUTH DEVON COLL. LIB.

83746	296·437
ACC.............	CLASS ....

Contents

It's spring again

PASSOVER takes place in the spring. It lasts for a week, but the main event is a special meal, called the seder meal.

Jerusalem, in Israel, is the centre of Judaism, the religion of Jewish people.

LOOKING BACK, AND FORWARD

Passover is a time when Jewish people look back to important events in their history. It is also a time when they look forward to the future, in the hope of better times to come. The festival dates back more than 3000 years and it reminds Jews of the the time when they were slaves in Egypt and God freed them from slavery. This event is called the Exodus. It is written about in the book of the Bible called Exodus.

6

FAMILY FUN

Jews usually share this festival with their family, and children especially have a lot of fun. Some families invite needy Jews to share their seder meal if they have nowhere else to go. Everything changes in Jewish homes at Passover - the food is different, and even the plates, cutlery and glasses are different from the rest of the year. People greet each other by saying 'Hag Sameach', which means 'A joyous festival' in Hebrew. Jewish children all over the world learn Hebrew so they can read the Bible in the language in which it was written.

The centre of the Jewish world is Jerusalem, in Israel. Passover, which is also called Pesach, begins when the new moon is seen in Jerusalem, and everyone prepares for the seder meal.

▲ Two Jewish boys reading Hebrew

A Jewish family enjoying the seder meal

Spring cleaning the house

EVERY YEAR when the time of Passover comes near, Jewish people know they must start to get the house ready from top to bottom.

FORBIDDEN FOODS

Springtime is traditionally a time of spring cleaning. For Jewish people, part of their spring clean is to clear out food that is not special for Passover. Jews do not eat 'leaven' foods during this festival. Leaven foods contain yeast, so most bread and biscuits are banned.

Children join in the search for leaven food, which the Jews call *hametz*. Some people leave a bit of *hametz* in each room so the children can look for it on the evening before the festival begins. In some families the children use a candle to see by, and a feather for brushing up the forbidden crumbs.

A candle and a feather are used to hunt out *hametz*.

ALL CHANGE!

In the kitchen the everyday pots and pans, plates and knives and forks are put away. Often, they are put away in a cupboard which is then sealed up for the eight days of the festival. Special crockery and cutlery are taken out and carefully washed ready for Passover.

On the day of the seder meal the table is carefully laid with the special Passover plates, knives and forks. Candlesticks are polished and flowers arranged. Everyone is looking forward to the evening celebrations.

Children at a Jewish primary school wash the cutlery ready for their seder meal.

A table set for the seder meal

9

Kosher cooking

ALL YEAR ROUND, Jews follow rules about what foods they eat and how they are cooked. At Passover, there are more special rules about their food.

A Jewish family in Israel enjoying an evening meal

FIT AND PROPER

Food that Jews are allowed to eat is called kosher, which means fit or proper. In the book of Leviticus, in the Bible, there is a list of animals that can be eaten. These animals are kosher. For example, Jews can eat any fish that has scales and fins, but they are not allowed to eat shellfish.

Kosher foods must be cooked in a certain way, too. One rule is that milk and meat must never be mixed together or eaten at the same meal,

Fish like these are kosher for Jews.

A mother and her daughter prepare a kosher meal.

so a beefburger followed by a yoghurt would not be allowed. In some Jewish homes, the kitchen has one part for cooking meats and another for cooking milk foods. So life is much easier for vegetarians!

A WEEK WITHOUT

At Passover, leaven food - food with yeast - is not allowed. Only unleavened food is kosher for Passover. Many Jews like to shop in Jewish stores where only kosher food is sold, but some supermarkets now sell kosher food too.

Shopping in a Jewish store

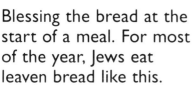 Baking bread and burning the hametz

B READ is an important part of most people's diet. At Passover, bread has a special meaning for Jews.

COOKING IN A HURRY

Passover is also called the Feast of Unleavened Bread. This is because only unleavened bread is eaten at this time. Bread without leaven (yeast) does not rise when it is baked, it stays flat. This kind of bread is called matzah. Matzah

Blessing the bread at the start of a meal. For most of the year, Jews eat leaven bread like this.

At Passover, Jews eat unleavened bread, called *matzah*.

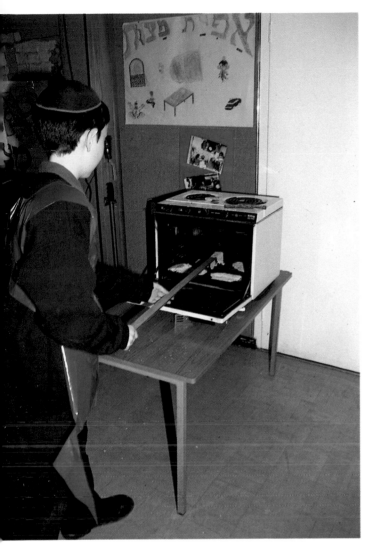

A schoolboy learns how to make *matzah*.

reminds Jews of the time long ago when Jews left Egypt. They had to leave in a hurry so they had no time to wait for their bread to rise.

FOOD IN THE FIRE

Just before Passover begins, children help their parents to burn any bits of leaven food, called *hametz*, which they have found in their search of the house. A small fire is lit outside the house and the *hametz* is burned. The father says a prayer to God. In his prayer he says he has done his best to clear out anything that should not be in the house during Passover.

The family is now ready for Passover to begin.

A fire is lit outside to burn the hametz.

13

Reading at the table

DURING THE PASSOVER MEAL, the story of the Exodus is told. The story is read from a special book called the Hagadah, which means 'telling'. It is written in Hebrew.

Everyone takes it in turns to read from the Hagadah

TAKING TURNS TO READ

When everyone sits down for the seder meal, they each have a book beside their plate. Even the children have their own Hagadah, which sometimes has pictures they have coloured in. People take it in turns to read a part of the story out loud. It takes a long time, so little children can stay up late for once!

Pharaoh, the Egyptian leader

PHARAOH THE SLAVE DRIVER

Our story begins long ago in Egypt. Pharaoh the Egyptian leader was worried about the large number of Jewish people there. He decided to make them slaves so that they could not harm him. He made them work long and hard. As more and more Jews were born, he decided that Jewish boys had to die.

One day, a mother hid her baby boy in some reeds so that the Egyptians could not kill him.

14

The Pharaoh's daughter found him and took him to her palace, where he grew up safely. He was named Moses, which means 'drawn out', because he was rescued from the river. As Moses grew up he saw how cruel the Egyptians were to the Jewish people.

THE BURNING BUSH

One day, Moses was so angry with an Egyptian that he hit him. The man died, so Moses had to escape. He left Egypt and worked as a shepherd in the deserts of Sinai.

Then a strange thing happened. He saw a bush on fire, but the bush was not harmed. Moses went to have a closer look. It was then that God told Moses to go to Pharaoh and say to him 'Let my people go.' So Moses went and told Pharaoh to free the slaves, but Pharaoh just laughed. So God sent some plagues on the Egyptians. (To find out the rest of the story, look on the next page!)

Some copies of the Hagadah, like this old one, are very beautiful.

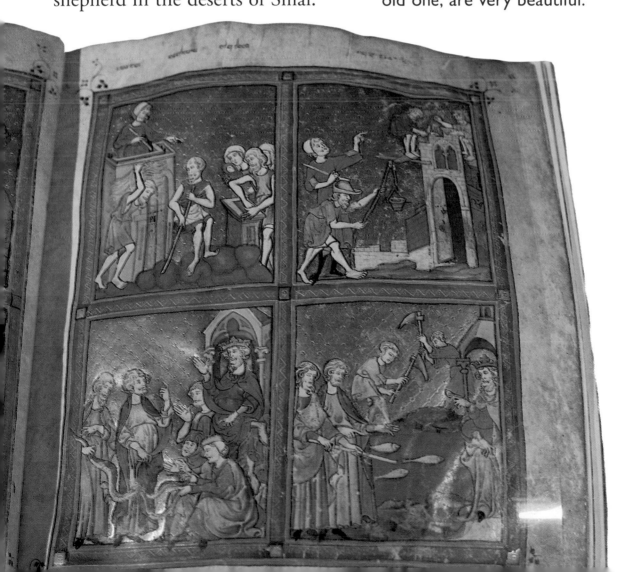

The story of the ten plagues

WHEN PHARAOH refused to set the slaves free, God made terrible things happen to punish the Egyptians. He sent ten different plagues which hurt the people, their animals and their crops.

WHAT NEXT?

The first plague that God sent turned the waters of the River Nile red. The fish died and the people could not drink the water, but Pharaoh would not let the Jews go.

The River Nile in Egypt, which turned red

So God made frogs come out of the Nile and swarm over the land, but Pharaoh would not let the Jews go.

So God sent a plague of lice across the country, but Pharaoh would not let the Jews go.

Next, God sent wild animals across the land, then a disease that killed the cattle, then a plague of boils, but Pharaoh would not let the Jews go.

Huge hailstones dropped from the sky, then a swarm of locusts ate the crops, then darkness came over the

The ten plagues in a modern Hagadah

16

land for several days, but still Pharaoh would not let the Jews go.

The tenth plague was the most terrible. The first son in every Egyptian family died.

After this last plague, Pharaoh let the people go.

THE FIRST PASSOVER MEAL

Before he sent the last plague, God had told the Jews to cook a meal of roast lamb, and to be ready to leave. They did not have time to make proper bread to take with them so they made flat bread that did not rise.

While the Jewish people ate their meal, the angel of death passed over their houses. Only the Egyptian sons were killed. This is why the festival is called Passover, because the angel passed over the houses of the Jews.

A page in a very old Hagadah, which shows the first Passover meal of roast lamb.

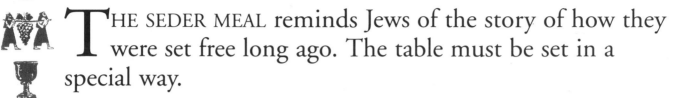

Setting the table for seder

THE SEDER MEAL reminds Jews of the story of how they were set free long ago. The table must be set in a special way.

A PLATE IN SIX PARTS

A seder plate is divided into six parts, for the six special foods that will be eaten. Each food is a symbol. First there is an egg, which is hardboiled and slightly roasted. It is a reminder of spring and new life, and of the temple in Jerusalem. Fresh herbs - usually parsley - are another reminder of spring, new life and hope. Bitter herbs remind the Jews of how bitter their slavery was. Lettuce reminds the Jews how good life was before they became slaves. The sweet taste of the lettuce becomes bitter after a few mouthfuls. *Haroset* is a mixture of apple and nuts. It is to remind the Jews of the mortar the slaves used when they were building. A shankbone, from a leg of lamb, reminds Jews of the temple where sacrifices were made to God.

A seder plate

18

WATER AND WINE

What else is on the table? Salt water, in which the parsley is dipped, is there to remind Jews of the tears of the slaves in Egypt. Wine is there, too. Even children have their own glass, which is filled four times during the meal. And in a separate dish are three pieces of matzah, the unleavened bread, under a special cover. Candles are lit to show the light and joy of the festival, and each seat has a pillow or cushion. Sitting in comfort reminds the Jews of their freedom. Last but not least, everyone has a copy of the Hagadah beside their plate.

Children have their own glass of wine.

The table is set for the seder meal.

The order of events

Seder means 'order'. The seder meal is eaten in a special order. There are fifteen parts to this Passover meal!

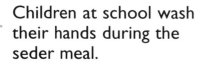

Children at school wash their hands during the seder meal.

Questions and answers

The children in the family learn about Passover by asking four questions during the meal. They ask 'Why do we eat only matzah? Why do we eat bitter herbs? Why do we dip parsley in salt water, and bitter herbs in the haroset? Why do we sit on a pillow?' Can you find the answers in this book?

Blessings

Jews always thank God before eating or drinking. Tonight, they start the meal by blessing the wine and drinking the first glass. During the meal they drink three more glasses of wine. Twice during the meal they stop to wash their hands in running water. They eat the foods from the seder plate in a set order, and at the end they sing songs and pray together. The seder includes a special meal. It will probably be the family's favourite foods, so long as they are kosher for Passover.

Hide and seek

Near the beginning of the meal, an adult hides a piece of matzah, which

Searching high and low for the *afikomen*

Found it!

is called the *afikomen*. Later the children go off to look for it. The meal cannot end until the *afikomen* has been found, so whoever finds it gets a prize!

WHERE'S ELIJAH?

Everyone eats a piece of the *afikomen*, and drinks a glass of wine. An extra glass is filled for the prophet Elijah, a Hebrew prophet. Jews believe he will one day return to Earth, and at Passover, children go to the door to see if he is on his way to their house.

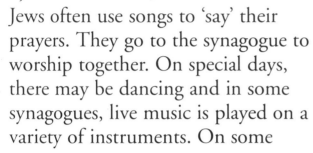 Psalms and songs

SↃONGS AND MUSIC are an important part of Jewish life and worship. At Passover, everyone joins in the singing during the seder meal - and afterwards, too!

SONGS IN THE SYNAGOGUE

Jews often use songs to 'say' their prayers. They go to the synagogue to worship together. On special days, there may be dancing and in some synagogues, live music is played on a variety of instruments. On some festival days, a traditional instrument is played - it is a shofar, made from a ram's horn, which is blown like a wind instrument.

Praying in the synagogue

SEDER SONGS

Near the end of the seder meal, most families sing some psalms together, from the Book of Psalms in the Bible. The psalms praise God and thank Him for his goodness. At this point in the meal, the fourth and last glass of wine is drunk.

People also like to sing traditional songs. One, called *Dayennu*, reminds Jews of all that God has done for them and helps them to count their blessings. After the meal, the singing may go on late into the night.

Children and teachers enjoying singing together at their seder meal at school

▲ Blowing a shofar

23

 The passing of Passover

D OES EVERYTHING RETURN to normal after the seder meal? Not quite!

A MEETING PLACE

The day after the seder meal is a holiday for Jews. Many Jews like to meet at the synagogue to pray and to celebrate Passover. Whenever Jews meet together for services, they read the Torah scrolls, which are their holy writings. The scrolls are kept in a cupboard called an ark. Each week they are taken out and the rabbi reads part of them. The next week he reads out the next part. It takes a year to read right through to the end like this.

The synagogue is the place of worship for Jews. But it can be other things, too. It can be a school where

A synagogue in Russia, where old friends like to meet.

An 18th-century synagogue in France (left) and (above) Torah scrolls kept in a cupboard called an ark.

children and adults go to learn Hebrew and to learn about Judaism. It can also be a place for friendship, where people worship together and make friends. And it is a special place at festival times, when Jews celebrate together.

BACK TO SCHOOL

Some people have a week's holiday at Passover and go out with their family, but most people go back to work, and children go back to school. For the rest of Passover, the main difference from the rest of the year is the food, which is still unleaven. And don't forget that the cutlery and crockery are different, too. When Passover comes to an end, they are wrapped up and put away for another year.

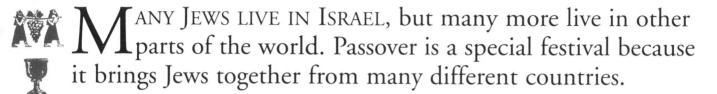 # 'Next year in Jerusalem'

MANY JEWS LIVE IN ISRAEL, but many more live in other parts of the world. Passover is a special festival because it brings Jews together from many different countries.

PASSOVER PILGRIMS

Israel is quite a new country, but Jews have lived in that part of the world for at least 3000 years. Today there are Jews in every continent of the world. They may speak different languages and wear different clothes, but wherever they live, they have one thing in common. They all think of Jerusalem, in Israel, as the central place of their religion.

Passover is an old 'pilgrim' festival. In the past pilgrim Jews travelled

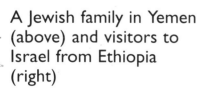

A Jewish family in Yemen (above) and visitors to Israel from Ethiopia (right)

from far and wide to celebrate the festival together in Jerusalem.

THE WESTERN WALL

Many years ago the Jews had a temple in Jerusalem where they worshipped God. The temple was destroyed by the Romans. All that remains is part of the outer wall. It is called the Western Wall. Jews travel to Jerusalem at special times in their lives, and at festivals such as Passover, to pray at the Western Wall.

Today, Jews all over the world say at Passover time 'Next year in Jerusalem'. For some, that wish comes true.

Praying at the Western Wall

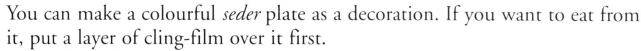 # Let's celebrate!

Join in the fun! Try making this *seder* plate and *haroset*. Use the pictures in this book to help you decorate the plate, and look on page 18 to find out about *haroset*.

MAKING A SEDER PLATE

You can make a colourful *seder* plate as a decoration. If you want to eat from it, put a layer of cling-film over it first.

You will need:

1 a paper plate
2 paints, crayons or felt-tip pens
3 coloured card or paper
4 PVA glue
5 safe scissors

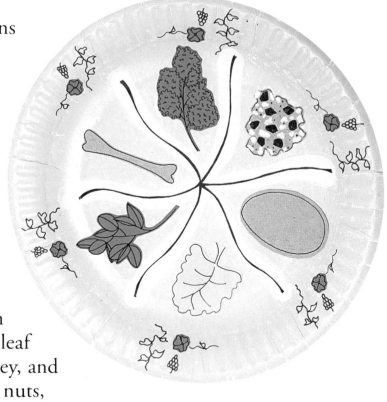

All you have to do is:

1 Paint the plate in a pale colour and let it dry.
2 Divide the plate into six sections with a pen.
3 Draw one of these shapes in each section or cut them out and stick them down: an egg, a bone, a bitter herb or leaf such as chicory lettuce, parsley, and *haroset* – a mixture of apple, nuts, cinnamon, honey and grape juice. Use the pictures in this book to help you.
4 Now decorate the plate with leaf patterns, flowers, bunches of grapes, olives, and so on.

Making Haroset

You will need:

1 four eating apples
2 a cup of nuts
3 a cup of sultanas or raisins
4 one level teaspoon of cinnamon
5 four tablespoons of grape juice

All you need to do is:

1 Peel and core the apples.
  Chop them finely or grate them.
2 Chop the nuts.
3 Mix all the ingredients together.

Glossary

Hagadah means 'telling'. The book used at Passover seder

Hag Sameach a Passover greeting meaning 'have a joyous festival'

hametz the last remaining pieces of leaven burnt before Passover begins

Hebrew the traditional language of Jewish scriptures and many Jews

Jerusalem the ancient city of David and capital of Israel today

kosher means 'fit' or 'proper'. Refers to foods allowed by Jewish dietary laws.

leaven substance which causes dough to ferment and rise eg. yeast

matzah flat bread, like a cracker. Used at Passover time

Pesach the Hebrew word for Passover. Festival celebrating the Exodus

seder means 'order'. Usually refers to the ceremonial meal in the home, eaten at Passover

synagogue a building set aside for Jewish public prayer, study and meeting together

Index

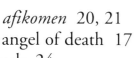